MW01226640

THE STRESS-FREE WORK DAY

How to Effectively Organize Your Day, Be Super
Productive, Increase Your Motivation, and Get
Out By 5!

JUSTIN BYERS

illustrative purposes only, are the property of their respective owners and not affiliated with this publication in any way. Any trademarks are being used without permission, and the publication of the trademark is not authorized by, associated with or sponsored by the trademark owner.

www.EmpowermentNation.com

Table of Contents

Introduction

Today's professional climates are fast-paced, complex, and rapidly changing. Professionals are constantly beset by a range of seemingly conflicting objectives and assignments. We're all too familiar with objectives that change on a daily or hourly basis, coupled with meetings that introduce new, seemingly garbled or confusing directions that can further confuse our situation. Many of us spend large portions of our day ruminating somewhat unpleasantly about the lack of communication between management and staff, or between team members.

If you are a member of the "walking dead," just holding on for retirement to roll around, such frustrations are merely that – daily job frustrations. But what if you aren't? What if you want increased productivity and a flourishing career? For an individual striving to increase her or his productivity in the professional field, such seemingly constant distractions and modifications to existing projects can quickly become overwhelming. How can you progress and advance professionally if anything you do requires a major overhaul the very next day?

Managers and corporate leaders often see

this problem from the flip side. Often times, coordinating projects that involve many people requires massive compromises from one department or another. Business leaders must make this call, and many are accustomed to grumblings and complaints from staff members as a result. Getting things done as a manager does require a bigger-picture perspective, to be sure, and it's not uncommon for people in these situations to feel overwhelmed by the forces at play.

Both situations are really two sides of the same coin. The larger reality is this: any business, corporation, et cetera, has a finite amount of resources available. Members of any staff are likely to see their resources slighted or undervalued by a decision that undoes some of their respective contribution to a project, while managers may become annoyed with certain departments or individuals for always complaining about necessary sacrifices.

The purpose of this book is to help guide all professionals towards greater levels of productivity and efficiency in the workplace. A few very simple habits can be adopted for exactly this purpose. None of them are very difficult, at least at first glance. Remember, old habits die hard, and it might be safer to take a period of several work weeks to master each productivity technique, but all of them will greatly increase your workplace efficiency.

Your Path to Productivity

You begin these exercises by assessing your own outlook on work. What, for example, do you enjoy about it? Do you consider yourself a successful person? If you do, try to say why. How a person feels about his or her work is critical to one's productivity for this reason: the better we understand what we want out of a career, the better we will be able to go after it. Consider your coworkers in general. Some of us genuinely enjoy many of the people we work with, others can't stand them, and all the rest of us fall somewhere in between. Attitude may not be absolutely everything, but it certainly makes all the difference when trying to become more productive, especially in the standard chaos of a day at work.

This is no small challenge. But success is all about learning and attitude - it's not that life's winners and losers are born that way. It's not that certain people just have a magical ability to accomplish whatever they set out to do. Everything worth doing and achieving in life takes courage, dedication, patience, and a positive attitude. That there, are ways to learn how to become more productive in your life. No one is born inherently knowing how to accomplish their largest dreams. Certainly, an occasional person will figure it out on his or her own. They are the big successes we aspire to be, and it's possible, with a little mental adjustment and motivation, to embark on that journey. Increasing your workplace productivity requires you to plan with precision, learn with goal-oriented purpose, and accept temporary setbacks with grace and a playful attitude.

Success, One Day at a Time

Very few people on this earth manage to go to sleep at night having accomplished everything they set out to do that day. If they have, it's a good bet they haven't aspired to complete much to begin with. Do yourself a favor now and try to remember the last time you went to bed satisfied that you'd accomplished a sizeable fraction of what you'd set out to on a given day. It may take a few moments, but try to remember a day when things went well, and perhaps only a minor task or two fell through the cracks of our best intentions.

Now consider your days in general. What is different about your lackluster days and those that really shine as successes? Was it luck? Did everything just fall into place without a single hitch? Were you driven by some desire to accomplish your tasks on the better day, while remaining generally uninspired on others? Perhaps, knowing the next day would be filled to the brim with daunting chores, you made a mental schedule of everything that would happen, and stuck to it the next day.

It is possible, with practice and patience, to manage day to day tasks with consistently higher levels of success, given the right understanding both of what happens when we are doing things right and what happens when we are not quite so task-oriented as we ought to be. Lost time adds up to minutes every hour, hours every day. If you practice the tips presented below, you can reasonably expect to experience an abundant increase in productivity. In less time than you'd imagine, these positive changes beget themselves in a self-encouraging fashion. Ending the day positively and successfully is a wonderful feeling, and will promote the same attitude and sense of direction in the next day, and the next, and so on. After all, wouldn't you love to begin every day with a set plan of action, a method for avoiding road blocks, and an overall sense of how today's productivity will enhance the next? The amount of time saved in a given day can invariably be used in turn to complete further assignments and perhaps assume even more responsibilities in the workplace.

Increasing your workplace productivity represents a commitment, and the more you want out of life, the more you'll simply have to commit to this change. All the tips, insights and suggestions in this book won't do a person any good if he or she is unwilling to follow through with making real changes to his or her life. Much of the advice is practical and represents a wealth of knowledge that simply gets overlooked or forgotten in the day-to-day bustle. A good example of something about productivity that we may not even know *we know*: we begin most new and engaging tasks with a burst of enthusiasm and productivity. Anywhere from a fifth to a third of the way through, we begin to feel as though we are too far away from our objective to possibly be successful.

Then, generally about halfway through, we find ourselves reinvigorated and determined to finish, brimming with new insights and ideas. We complete another ten percent of the task — and suddenly we feel as though we are farther away from reaching the goal than we ever were. We struggle and scramble for progress until we are around ninety percent complete with the task. With the end in sight, the completion of whatever we set out to accomplish seems inevitable, and almost effortless. This is true of almost anything we set out to achieve, regardless of whether it is a marathon, learning to play a musical instrument, or writing a novel. Somehow, we humans go through the same meta-procedures in the accomplishment of tasks, regardless of what the task may actually entail. Knowing this can prevent you from turning away from your goals — if you find yourself feeling stuck after about a third of a large goal, good! That's how you're supposed to feel. With that in mind, why not keep going with it and see what happens next?

Everyone who manages to accomplish great things does so by following the same essential set of rules and guidelines. They understand the principle of motivational processing outlined above. They have trained themselves to forgo a large number of leisurely activities that eat up time disproportionate to the amount of fulfillment they can provide. They accept setbacks and errors as opportunities for learning and personal growth, and they do not accept failure. They know what they want, and they are unswerving in their determination to get it. Knowing how the minds and techniques of productive individuals work can allow us to mimic their ways and obtain our own goals. In the workplace, productivity flows best when projects are as simplified as possible, and people completing those projects remain as focused on completion as possible.

Focus on the Positive

The most important aspect of productivity in the workplace is the constant maintenance of attention directed to the task at hand. It is very easy to let yourself become bogged down in negative attitudes or distracting conversations, especially if a project isn't going well or has suddenly stopped making sense to a large number of people. The most common reaction to this is a sudden sea of bad talk, gossip, and negativity.

It happens. Let it happen, but make an effort to play no role in it. If you wish to be productive, there is no worse application of your time and resources than to come up with reasons why nothing is going to work out right. This is even more true for large projects, where every individual seems to believe he or she has best vision for the project. If changes do occur and they don't immediately make sense to you (they almost never will, if your office is anything like the majority of offices on earth), the first question you need to answer is this: *Why should it make sense to me?*

If you are in a position where the change should seem sensible, then you are obligated to address this concern with management. Often times, though, team members may feel automatic resistance or disdain for changes. Perhaps, a moment's thought can put things back into perspective. Accept your share of what needs to be accomplished, stay focused on that, and move on. It's natural enough to want to understand the bigger picture of a large project, but part of being productive and staying so will require focus. For the workplace, this means do what is required of you as best as you can, and allow everyone else to do the same.

Resist the Negative!

We can spend endless energy complaining about what is going wrong on any project. To stay productive, remain disengaged from that trend within the office. It may seem nice (at least initially) to converse with coworkers in this fashion, especially if everyone appears to be similarly flustered, but aside from wasting time, this type of conversation can actually make things worse than they really are. Negativity does have a certain gravity about it. Bickering and bemoaning in the office usually takes on a life of its own, and can make once manageable problems or issues into tremendous challenges. The more people who stay focused (and staying positive is a big part of staying focused), the less these negative outlooks tend to accrue. Below are listed a few simple techniques for avoiding negative discourse in the workplace.

Leave the room: If you can, suddenly find a better place to be. This obviously won't be possible in every situation, especially if the room you need leave is your office, but you can suddenly "realize" that you have to complete something right away, or realize your attention is needed on some other issue, in order to withdraw from a negatively-focused conversation.

It is important to be polite about this. A large part of staying professional in the workplace does include respecting the feelings of your coworkers, and gruff dismissals of one or two coworkers can quickly pile up to a reputation as someone who is 'unfriendly' or 'cold.' Such a reputation will always make things more difficult in the long run, especially in circles of coworkers who have been together for years. A large part of productivity in the workplace involves effective communication, and that will be difficult to achieve if those around you have difficulty approaching you. In situations where you sense negative talk beginning to occur, it's always handy to have several pre-thought out reasons why you might suddenly need to disengage from a conversation. Even better, if you have a constructive way of reframing the situation, voice that assertively and respectfully.

Stay Silent: This is surprisingly effective in groups of four or more people. If complaints start piling up in a group of people, you are often free to continue your own work unhindered, and you are not required to stop what you're doing to chip in your two cents, as it were. The most likely scenario is that no one will notice. They may assume a tacit agreement from you, but that's their problem. You've got work to do in any case.

It's very common in the workplace to join in a conversation seemingly for its own sake. Never feel obligated to bad-mouth policies or people you work with on a regular basis. The primary reason being, you work with them, and if you wish to increase your productivity, you'll need to develop relationships in the office that benefit you and your goals, you'll only be hindering yourself from progress by doing so. This can ruin people's reputations as well, since the same negativity that can unravel projects can also be directed at coworkers in much the same way. Refrain from this kind of talk, and in some cases you'll even find the person under fire is perfectly capable of his or her job. Even in cases where this is not the case, it's never a good idea to go out of your way to speak poorly about someone in the workplace.

Be the Example: Perhaps your workplace or office has a worker or two with a reputation for being an effective communicator and relatively drama-free. Consider what makes this person so appealing to work with. Follow his or her example, and try to be it. Following a positive example will allow you to change the dynamic of the office as well as your own work habits.

There's a secret teachers know about their

classrooms, some of you will no doubt be familiar with from your days in grade school. A seemingly-rowdy group of students can have its entire dynamic changed by something as simple as a change in seating arrangements. If two particularly chatty students are seated next to one another, they have a tendency to set off the entire classroom. This principle, interestingly enough, carries over into adult life. However, your bosses are far from likely to consider changing seating arrangements because of negative practices adopted in the workplace. Honestly, they shouldn't have to—we're adults, and we ought to be able to control our behavior better than when we were third-graders. We simply forget to exert self-control at times, and this can lead to less than optimal working conditions for everyone.

You have the power to make significant changes in attitudes around the workplace with small changes in your own behavior. This isn't to say that up until now you were a big part of the problem—not by a long shot. It's simply very true that engaging in workplace gossip can happen almost before you're aware of it. Talk is easy, but fortunately there are also easy tips to stop yourself from engaging in talk that might detract from your own goal of increased productivity in the workplace.

The easiest thing to do is to ask yourself how you would feel if someone walked in on a conversation you were having. Are there people you would suddenly change the subject around, or who would make you feel suddenly uncomfortable? If so, it's a good bet you should bring the conversation to a quick close or change the subject to something positive—something productive—since complaining won't accomplish much of anything at all. Your coworkers will get the hint quickly enough that you won't have to do this for very long. People who engage in gossip do so to reinforce their own negative feelings about a person or situation. If they can't get that from you, they'll stop trying after a while.

It's fair enough to openly ask your coworkers to stop engaging in gossip too, if it's a major problem in your workplace. It is, after all, far too easy for things to become misinterpreted or exaggerated as they spread from person to person, and misunderstandings of this sort compound quickly enough that rumors typically degenerate into baseless claims. If you voice these and other concerns about gossip-related conversations your coworkers are having, you're making it clear that you don't want that kind of activity around you.

It's also a good idea to take stock of your own style and prior accomplishments. Determine what sorts of things motivate you towards success. Goals are great, but in order to achieve them you'll need to remind yourself why. If you want to make more money, imagine what having that extra money will feel like. If you desire success for its own sake, find ways to remind yourself as you work that you're working towards success. Whatever reasons you have for becoming more productive in your professional life, surround yourself with ways to access that motivation. Don't be afraid to change things up, and frequently if need be. For example, if a certain phrase or thought is placed somewhere in your office in order to motivate you, and you find it isn't doing the trick, perhaps you've outgrown that phrase or have gotten everything you need from it. Find something to replace it, do what you need to do in order to stay motivated towards your goals. We'll have more tips for this in a later section.

Address the Negative, When Needed

You've begun taking steps to ensure that you aren't responsible for lost time or resources by complaining about inevitable changes or frustrations, and it's fair that you expect the same from those you work with. Again, it's important not to make things personal, but we all know a coworker (past or present) who found regular ways to poison your shared work environment. This person represented a constant distraction and drain on those around him or her. If no one ever figured out how to deal with that person (too often, the case), you know how destructive it was. Be prepared to make sure you are not similarly bogged down in the future.

If someone is a consistent workplace irritant, you should deal with the problem. Address the situation in terms of what you are feeling as opposed to what that person is doing that you consider inappropriate. Do this as soon as possible — delaying address of any given situation can only make things potentially worse. Make your concerns as clear and non-hostile as humanly possible. Allow the person you are addressing the opportunity to redress these concerns in a polite way—if any unprofessional behavior begins at this point, it's evidence that you were correct to address the situation.

Once you have addressed the situation, allow several days to reassess the situation. Is your coworker still engaging in these same undesirable behaviors? If so, it may be time to readdress the situation with higher-ups. Frame the problem in terms of how it disrupts the work of those around you and be sure both the bothersome coworker and anyone else who needs to be involved has a clear idea of what your complaint is. Don't focus it on how it makes you feel or how it makes others feel—stay on message and stick to why the given behavior is disruptive in the workplace. Dealing with difficult coworkers is – by definition – difficult, and the nature of the coworker's disruption can take a wide range of forms. Whatever the case, if something occurring at work is disrupting your ability to accomplish tasks, the chances are it's not just you who is being sidetracked.

Deal with Unprofessional Professionals

It's possible that a coworker can manage to disrupt your productivity while remaining within the bounds of professionalism. This can put you in something of a bind—it makes approaching superiors for help with the problem unwise. However, the list of techniques below can help you manage the problem, or at least reduce it as much as possible. Always remember, in the context of a workplace situation, professionalism is critical. Diplomacy is a matter of course, and it will be on you to take the extra step to make sure you take your problem-coworker's feelings into account as you address the situation.

Spend as much time as necessary to deal with the problem and not a second more. Constantly trying to quell unprofessional coworkers can drain resources very quickly. Also make sure not to go out of your way to deal with a problem that isn't your problem. If, for example, you begin hearing that a coworker has begun excessive gossiping, it might seem important to address the situation with that coworker directly, especially if the gossip concerns you! However, if it isn't directly related to professional conduct, and cannot really affect you or your work in a negative way, it might be better just to let the gossiper's reputation slip away of its own accord. Here are some common types of problems created by coworkers in the office:

Complainers: These coworkers complain about a wide range of things, from the situation in the workplace to their family, if they are particularly off-task. They might also be constant complainers about their back or leg, or neck pains, and these conversations can often absorb the majority of their days. The complaint is their primary method of communication with others. They've learned it's attention getting, and it comes naturally to them. It's important to note that they can burn a lot of time you're trying to spend being productive. They'll often engage in conversations with others for the sole purpose of expressing a complaint in detail, and if you're interested in increasing your productivity in a workplace shared with such coworkers, it is generally a good idea to avoid them as much as possible.

Failing that, try to counter what they have

to say with positive (and polite) responses. If you know they are about to complain about something, you might try interrupting them with a sudden burst of positivity. For example, if you have a new department head, and the complainer begins to speak about him or her, cut the complainer off by saying something along the lines of "I like our new department head. He/she brings a fresh perspective I've been looking forward to," or some such optimistic appraisal. It doesn't necessarily need to be true; your mission here is to curb the complainer's proclivity towards negative talk in the future, at least as far as it concerns you. If you get good enough at cutting them off at the pass, you can look forward to less and less approaches from these coworkers in the future. They generally aren't interested in anything constructive, so you'll be allowed to continue your work unbothered by them.

Another sound tactic you might want to try is offering a genuine solution or a way to go about solving a problem that a complainer has presented to you. For all we've said against complainers in this section, it's a fair reminder that some people do need to rely on the help of others from time to time. That's true for all of us, so if you have knowledge or insight into a complainer's problem — a work related one, preferably — try sharing it. If you help the person — great. If he or she comes up with several immediate reasons why your suggestion won't work, it's a good bet the complainer wasn't looking for genuine assistance in the first place.

Gossipers: Very similar to complainers, gossipers frequently speak about other people, typically coworkers, in a negative way. Gossipers tend to exaggerate, pick targets according to who is least likely to defend themselves, and distort what is really going on in the workplace. The comments are often work related, although gossips about someone's personal life can be just as damaging in the workplace. They also tend to inspire other people to gossip, and will continue to spread negative comments until the entire office has an inaccurate impression of the gossiper's targets.

Gossipers should either be avoided or addressed directly as such, especially if the gossip is entirely inappropriate (which, by definition, it usually is). Always be wary of conversations that might head down this road. Gossip tends to be interspersed with work-related subjects, at least at first, but can quickly dominate the conversation if the gossiper is present. To this end, don't be afraid to stop the talk in its tracks and recover the conversation, especially if it contains information important to your work.

If you realize that someone in the office has been gossiping about you, you are well within your rights to either confront the person or advance the issue to your supervisor. Be clear about what the person is saying, how it detracts from a professional environment, and that you expect the behavior to be eliminated as soon as possible. If it continues, get a journal ready and keep notes on everything you've heard about the gossip. Please note, however, that gossip can often be disproportionately frustrating. A person with a solid working relationship with many of her or his coworkers has, in reality, very little to actually fear from gossip. Keeping a record of the things you are hearing is only necessary when you firmly believe that your career or someone else's career is at stake. The journal will make it easier to confront the person or deal with them in an otherwise professional manner. And do be sure to keep it professional — can't be very productive in the workplace without professionalism.

Over-E-mailers: These are the people who compose an e-mail relevant to only a few people in the office and then blast it out to the entire workforce. Worse, they may send pictures of their pets, children, weekend excursions, etc. With most office inboxes already overloaded, this kind of clutter is unwelcome and distracting, especially if you are expecting important documents to arrive in your inbox. You can't just flag this coworker's e-mail as spam, either, because he or she might occasionally send an e-mail your way that requires your attention. That means you're left to delete plenty of unwanted e-mail, but first you have to sort through what is relevant and what isn't. This is time consuming, and all of us have better ways to spend our time than becoming our own spam filters.

Typically, the best way to deal with an over-e-mailer is to forward the unwanted e-mail to your supervisor, and ask the supervisor to deal with the situation. Most will comply, because company e-mail is supposed to be used for company purposes only. Failing that, you may need to send the e-mailer an e-mail yourself, explaining that you want to see only work-related materials to your e-mail account. Explain that you are waiting to receive several important reports (or whatever your basic reason is) and don't want to sort through personal or unwanted materials. It might be a good idea to explain that your desire to receive only professional e-mail isn't personal, but that you are presently far too busy to engage in any other types of e-mail exchange.

Another word here is necessary with respect to e-mailing in the office. Recent advances have allowed us to better manage correspondence. Many e-mail servers are able to determine whether senders intended to attach a document, or detect the absence of a recipient who usually receives certain types of correspondence. It's not flawless, but it is very helpful. Whatever the case may be with your e-mail in the workplace; be very mindful that many careers have been ruined in the blink of an eye by those "advances." For example, you might send a coworker a report that contains negative or controversial information. That report could accidently be forwarded to your supervisor or another coworker as part of an e-mail string. Keep this in mind whenever you write e-mails of a professional nature. Any negativity in them can cause serious issues down the road.

A related problem with e-mail is the supervisor who relies too heavily on it for coordination. A conversation consisting of e-mail quickly becomes opaque and inoperable. Sometimes the best way through a problem or project is through direct communication, and that means face-to-face meetings, group discussions, et cetera. Dealing with an employer or supervisor who shuns direct contact with the people he or she depends on is possibly the greatest challenge in the workplace. They aren't breaking any specific rules, and to an extent, it's their prerogative how they wish to manage things. On the other hand, if a project desperately needs consensus and direction, a meeting is mandatory.

Address that reality as tactfully as possible, in an e-mail if necessary. Make it known that you're very excited for the project and would like time for the entire group to sit down and discuss it as a whole. A well-organized meeting can accomplish a great deal more than serial e-mails where facts and input get muddled and confused.

The Obnoxious: The obnoxious coworker engages in some kind of activity that most reasonable people perceive as obnoxious, and it's a difficult problem to solve. Different types of behavior might include constant throat-clearing, sighing, knuckle-cracking, finger tapping, or leg jiggling. The reason these coworkers might be more difficult to deal with lie in the types of activity they engage in. It's not necessarily a good idea to complain to a supervisor that so-and-so is constantly sighing and that makes it difficult for you and others to concentrate, even if it is true. It's much tougher for a boss to confront a coworker about these types of behavior, for the most part, so you'll have to make due in some smaller way. At the very least, you might have to resolve to yourself that you simply won't let the behavior get to you, and any time it occurs, remind yourself of that decision.

If the behavior gets out of control, be very tactful in how you approach the wording of your complaint. In some cases, sighing for example, the person sighing isn't even aware he or she is doing it, and maybe drawing attention to the behavior will be all that's required to end it, or at least curb it. That's all the more reason not to jump in with something like "I can't concentrate with you sighing, all the time." You might instead say something like "Are you okay? Because I notice you've been sighing a lot lately." That way, you've taken care of the problem without really confronting the person at all.

The Perfume/Cologne Wearer: Some people have no idea how much scented product they should wear. This is partly true because we tend to have widely varying sensitivities to smell, but for whatever reason, certain fragrances can overpower some of us quite easily if they are liberally applied. In the most extreme cases, overpowering smells can cause nausea or allergic reactions. In many ways, this problem may be the toughest one to deal with in the workplace. There might be a dress code and rules about noise regulation, but it's much rarer that the nature of scent is addressed directly. If the scent becomes too much of a problem for you, you'd probably be best served finding another scent to mask it and keep it nearby. If that doesn't work, you'll have to talk to the person directly about your problem. This a very good time to be extra-sensitive of his or her feelings. Don't address this in front of other people, for example, as that can cause further and unnecessary embarrassment. If the problem centers on a genuine health concern, be sure to say so — your coworker will be far more likely to take the news well. These are common issues with employees who are pregnant or have sensitive allergies. Whatever the case may be, reasonably clear air is important for productivity. Ask for less perfume or cologne if you must.

Pranksters: This coworker is always joking, pulling pranks, and apparently never serious. He or she has usually become permanently distracted in an ongoing attempt to get laughs and approval from everyone else. The end result is a workforce distracted by constant antics. This is another trouble area when it comes to dealing with problem coworkers. Essentially, there's nothing wrong with having a sense of humor, and honestly, if the so-called prankster is judicious enough to make people laugh without significantly disrupting the work atmosphere, he or she is likely doing more good than harm. However, this is seldom the case. Attempting to make people laugh in the workplace is totally fine, but racially, sexually, or otherwise inappropriately charged comments can quickly deteriorate into serious trouble for the careless. Equally disruptive is when an overbearing prankster decides to target certain individuals in his or her workplace. How can anyone get work done if they are busy wondering when and where the next zinger will strike?

Bullies: Similar to pranksters, but never acceptable in the workplace. Bullies are mean-spirited as opposed to playful. They often yell at coworkers, attempt to humiliate or embarrass them, or otherwise attempt to gain power over them. Insults and negative comments are very common, and they may be of a personal nature. With bullies, documentation is key. No person engaging in this kind of behavior should be allowed in your workplace, and documentation will be useful to a supervisor looking into such allegations. Seek input and coordinate your documentation with others who have witnessed it or been victims of it. Don't confront the bully directly — a person with a proclivity towards aggressive behavior is highly unlikely to change on the basis of one conversation. Always involve supervisors or employers in the confrontation. Odds are that the bully has far more experience attacking and tearing down others than you do confronting such people in a constructive fashion.

Also important note is that many bullies suffer from psychological problems, ranging from personality disorders to bi-polar disorder. Getting through to people with such conditions requires the focus of mental health professionals, and by their very nature, bullies with such conditions will not be receptive to constructive feedback on their communication skills. Bullies attempt to assert power over others by using abusive means and are often very skilled at bypassing rational requests or approaches. Rather than putting yourself in the position of experiencing further bullying, it's probably best to let the higher-ups deal with the situation.

Empty Promisors: These coworkers come in two types. They either agree to your requests and then fail to deliver, or they make expansive offers or commitments and don't uphold them. People may behave this way for a wide range of reasons. Maybe they can't say no to projects or requests when they simply do not have enough time to complete them. Maybe they are too disorganized and lack a consistent system for following through with agreements.

Empty promisors are particularly destructive to productivity when you have time constraints. If you expect to receive a report in two days, for example, you will likely base your schedule on that expectation. When the report does not show up, you're in trouble. This can be especially difficult to deal with when the needs of a particular project changes often, as incoming communications between team-members can become jumbled and reprioritizations occur. If gentle reminders are not enough to get the empty promisor to complete a task, you could be in for the long haul. True, passing delinquencies on to a supervisor might be regarded as tattling, but if the empty promisor is severely impairing your ability to work, such a step might be necessary.

Sometimes, you can recognize a person as someone who makes grandiose commitments and fails to deliver, and just ignore whatever he or she promises you. It's all too easy to fall behind in today's workplace, but empty promisors have turned non-delivery into an art-form. If the problem persists from one of your coworkers, address the problem with them briefly and professionally, and if that fails, you'll have to move on.

Slackers: These coworkers never carry their weight in the office. They consistently miss deadlines, shirk their responsibilities, and have a propensity for taking credit where none is due. They are similar to empty promisors, but are generally too slack to make promises in the first place. Slackers disrupt the workplace by failing to do their fair share of the work, leaving you and other productive coworkers to compensate for their lack of commitment. As with most of the other forms of disruptive or distracting coworkers, documentation is of primary importance when dealing with them. Supervisors don't want anyone unwilling to do the hard bogging down the team, and indeed most team-members will readily disapprove of a slacker's behavior.

If someone in your office is continually failing to produce measurable progress in a project or assignment, begin writing it down. Emphasize facts —missed deadlines and uncompleted aspects of the projects that the coworker is responsible for. Be ready for the person you are complaining against to cite one or two examples of someone else's failure to justify their own incomplete assignments. Remember, that's not the issue. It's common for people in a team to fall behind here and there — a typical coworker is just as swamped as you are, and sometimes a brief reminder is sufficient to recover a needed piece of work. Slackers will attempt to make the most out of this reality, but rather than taking it as a sign that they still have work yet to be completed, they will attempt to use it as an excuse to accomplish far less than you and your coworkers.

Make the Right Friends

True, work isn't a popularity contest and shouldn't be treated that way. That doesn't mean socialization is always undesirable, and in fact it can be very productive. At the same time you look for people or habits in the workplace that can disrupt and impede your goals, make sure to spend just as much time and effort seeking to improve your own work quality and habits by adopting methods and attitudes of those around you whom you respect. If you're having trouble completing assignments on time, take care to notice workers who are able to complete their work in a timely fashion, and try to determine what they are doing that works so well. If someone always has something constructive to say, pay attention to how she or he phrases it. You can trust that other people in your workplace desire to increase their productivity just as much as you. (At least, there should be!) Surrounding yourself with like-minded individuals will help you stay motivated, and give you the added benefit of being able to share experiences and bounce ideas off some and request feedback from others. Creating this type of professional atmosphere will go a long way towards eliminating negative or unproductive energies around you in countless ways. Perhaps you've had this experience, for example: you've looked at a problem or situation a dozen different ways, and cannot come up with a satisfactory solution. You remark about the problem and its seeming hopelessness to a friend or coworker, who instantly solves it for you. We all get stuck in ruts, and we can all be brought out of these ruts by people around us.

Use Your Time Productively

Free as Much Time as You Can

Not surprisingly, you'll need to "free up" as much time as you can at the office in order to stay productive. What this really means is that you'll need to streamline all of the available time you has as efficiently and effectively as possible.

Get it in writing: Highly productive individuals know what they want, and they've very likely got it written down somewhere. This habit cannot be stressed enough. It is far too easy for us to become sidetracked if we haven't clearly identified for ourselves precisely what we are planning to accomplish. It's common enough in the workplace that projects or objectives become so muddled or piled up that you can lose track of what needs to be done when. An important skill to foster and maintain in the office is the ability to determine what things actually need to get done versus what can be set aside for a later date, or left incomplete altogether.

How many of us, for example, have bosses or administrators who constantly change their minds with respect to small details of a project? More importantly, you may find yourself asked to complete pieces of a project or to compile something that will be forgotten the moment the task is assigned. It can be tricky at first to determine what is actually expected of you and what is only mentioned offhand. It might be useful at first to keep track of all the things you're asked to do in, say, a week. Take note of what was needed and what was effectively discarded. You might be surprised at how much time you spend on things of little significance because your employer or supervisor asked you to. If that turns out to be the case, continue with the task log. At some point, you'll want to address your concern directly, in the context of company time and resources.

If you can come up with a daily to-do list at work of three things that you need to accomplish, and accomplish those three things, believe it or not, you're doing an excellent job. This may sound counterintuitive — accomplishing only three tasks per day sounds tremendously ineffective at first, but if you continue to log your tasks, you'll find that three important things a day is a solid goal that can take you far. It's very common for us to start out the day taking on eight or nine tasks, and by the end we've been distracted or derailed so many times we've accomplished none, and only managed to start a few. Your attention deserves your attention, so to speak. It will be up to you to learn where to direct your effort and input to maximal effect. This will take persistence and patience, and there's no way around it but through.   This can be a great reason to look for kindred spirits in the office. If someone else is struggling to become more productive, you will be able to assist her or him and receive assistance in return. With this in mind, it's a good bet to search around your workplace for people experiencing the same difficulties you are. How successful you become will depend almost completely on your determination.

Also, take careful note of things you've completed successfully in the past. You may not be surprised to learn that you've done similar or related tasks at work many, many times before you set out to accomplish something larger. Think about the times that you have done so and come up with several reasons you were able to. Write them down somewhere — the most effective tool will be a simple and small notebook. Trying to computerize this process sounds appealing at first, but what we are aiming for here is simplicity. Files can get lost on computers.

Develop goals for the workplace. What do you want out of increased productivity? Avoid the pitfall of deciding you want something like more money just because you can't think of anything else to want. Be totally honest with yourself, and go for broke. If money is something you want more of, and it probably is, run with that. But does something else interest you more? Maybe you believe you see a better way to structure your workplace. It could also be that a particular task or process used commonly in your workplace strikes you as inefficient or outdated. Take a look and see. If you know of other similar places that do these things better than your own office, look at what works for them and begin building a proposal to change things over.

Most of the things you've written down are probably things that you want to gravitate *towards*. Many of you will have written things like "a new house" or "a better paying job" or "higher golf score." Now comes the part where you consider what motivated you to do similar things in the past. An overwhelming section of the population does not make significant changes in order to move towards positive goals. That is to say, most of us don't make an attempt to do something because it's what we want to do. Instead, we usually move away from things that we don't want: we try to avoid negative consequences. The reasons for this most common decision-making process is unclear, but think of the task of losing weight. Most often, people begin healthier practices not in order to improve their already stellar constitution, but rather because they want to improve their health or physique. Perhaps, they were instructed to do so by their care provider.

This way of making decisions and allotting time — avoiding displeasure as opposed to actively seeking pleasure — is not by any means an inferior outlook on life. And how could it be, if so many of us adopt this point of view? When seeking new undertakings, especially something like increasing your own productivity in the workplace, it's a great idea to identify the things that can go wrong — and things will, from time to time.

The first thing to establish what makes you tick:

- Are you one of the rare people who gravitates towards new tasks and professional goals with ease? If so, when you visualize yourself obtaining new skills or completing objectives you've established, you will experience a much greater ease in appreciating the results.

- If you tend to avoid displeasure, you will need to come up with goals and objectives that emphasize the fact that you wish to move away from something that is presently bothering you. In this case, something like "promotion" will need to be rephrased into "getting out from under my current job." This is because an idea like "promotion" will invariably come weighted with stress and unpleasant possibilities, and if you are geared to avoid unpleasantness, it's always a good idea to emphasize any discomfort you are presently feeling.

In terms of wanting a new promotion, this means you need to identify the reasons why you want to leave your old position. Get fed up. Don't get fed up with yourself, or with others unless it will genuinely benefit you to do so, but get fed up at situations, things that you do out of sheer habit, and perhaps even that your present circumstances aren't as bright as you deserve. Use that energy to make something happen about it. As time progresses and you get more successes under your belt, you'll naturally begin to gravitate towards new objectives as opposed to avoiding unpleasant situations. Because you'll become more familiar with positive outcomes, you'll become more familiar with the positive feelings they inherently elicit. Eventually, you'll be forward-oriented in the accomplishment of your goals, confident in the knowledge that your work and determination is getting you somewhere.

The secret to identifying goals in this fashion involves turning the unpleasant situation or possibility into something to strive for. If you are the type of person who tries to avoid displeasure and undesirable circumstances, you have a great arsenal of motivation at your disposal. For example, if someone at work or in your social circle behaves in a way that you find unacceptable, you suddenly have a concrete and obtainable goal right in front of you. Why not, in this case, set a goal for yourself to deal with this person in a way that will remove the problem in a fair and beneficial way? If you find yourself constantly distracted by unnecessary phone-calls or e-mails, why not set a goal to find a way to reduce or eliminate them altogether? With a minimal amount of thought, you can turn anything you wish to avoid into a goal you wish to achieve. This is really the same thing as identifying things that we want, it just takes a slight modification and we have something positive to strive for.

Motivated and productive people are incredibly skilled at avoiding time-wasting activities. It's impossible to increase your productivity while keeping the basic structure of your work day the same. This restructuring of your routine must consist of identifying and eliminating activities that do not progress your goals. This end requires discipline and sometimes may require significant adjustment, but there's substitute for freeing up more time to be productive if that's really what you want.

Avoid the Rush: If you can get to work early, by all means, do so. A half-hour before the majority of the rest of the staff has come in will guarantee you uninterrupted time when you can get things done. It's tempting in the mornings to spend a while conversing with coworkers about non-work related subjects. You can have a great deal of work accomplished by the time those distractions arrive, and you'll likely be in the middle of something by the time the office is full, making you less inclined to join in small talk.

If you can't arrive early, you can still arrange your day so that you avoid likely distractions. Take note of things around the office and make an effort to see when the break room is most full (that is to say, when breaks are most likely for you and the staff-members inside the break room to run long). Perhaps you can stay fifteen minutes extra at the end of your day, although this isn't recommended if it means you'll be even deeper in traffic. Proper timing can actually shorten your drive so that time you might lose with your family or otherwise at home won't be significantly impacted. Take a good look at whatever you can do throughout the day to avoid large groups of people conversing. Conversation might be entertaining, but if you're trying to become more productive in the workplace, they'll be a hindrance to you.

Have a plan: We tend to go through daily affairs with a general idea of what we need to do. Getting it in writing, scheduling times, and making sure we're sticking to things as much as possible will help in the development of professional productivity. It's too easy to forget a task here and there in order to leave something to chance on busy days. Active use of a daily or even an hourly planner will benefit you in countless ways. Reminders serve to ensure that we are aware we began our day with certain objectives and then additionally serve to remind us of our commitment to professional productivity. Write out the schedule the night prior. Glance at it and remind yourself what needs to be done as soon as you wake up. Take note of everything you intend to do. Take the schedule with you. Provide yourself with reminders of when you should be ending one task and starting another. Give yourself breathing room here and there just in case something gets in the way.

Eat in the office if you can. Going out for lunch means dealing with traffic or other stresses and can make you more disposed to engage in distractions when you return. Use the time you'd normally spend driving to a place to eat to relax and regroup. Set a timer to alert you to when your breaks occur and leave what you're doing as immediately as possible. Find something to do that relaxes you during your break. Idle activities that you find refreshing will work best for the most part. If there's a company break room, don't head right in simply because everyone else is there. These rooms might be the factory for company gossip, depending on who is there. Consider alternative break areas for yourself if this is indeed the case.

Create A Daily Schedule: Develop a schedule at work, and write it down. Otherwise, you've little more than a vague idea of what you want to achieve for the day. The reason that work is so dependent on scheduling is because it is an efficient way of managing time, and it's important to take this attitude with you wherever you go if you're trying to increase your efficiency and productivity. A clear schedule will help you avoid procrastination and time-distortion at once, since it will bestow upon you a delineated blueprint towards achieving your objectives. Start with when you arrive at work, and finish with when you plan to leave. Set timers for meetings, and when they go off, excuse yourself if you can. Do your utmost to stay on schedule. Some bosses or coworkers might be habitual over-talkers. If you must meet with them to discuss anything, make clear that your attention is needed elsewhere once the allotted time for the meeting ends. Draw their attention to the schedule and if they start to wander off subject, it will be your responsibility to redirect them.

Daily schedules can provide impetus to accomplish many tasks, but even with such an itinerary, it's still important to identify things that we gravitate towards in life. We all possess far more goals, regardless of how vague or undefined they might be, than we possess time to accomplish them. The more defined these goals are, the more likely we are to remember them, and the more likely we are to stick to them.

It won't be uncommon, especially at the beginning, to experience a massive disparity between what you think you can accomplish in one day and what actually gets done. Give yourself a modest work schedule at first, allowing yourself to make errors and adjustments as needed. As you get better at completing goals in the time you've given yourself, you can slowly add more to your schedule as you progress. Many people set out with twelve or thirteen things that they want to accomplish in a given day, only to find that perhaps as few as three were actually feasible. This is to be expected in the beginning, and in many ways it is the direct opposite of wondering where all the time in our day went. With a schedule written out, one can make notes regarding completion or progress of something, and save them over time.

It is always beneficial to go back and see what has actually been done in a day's or week's time to determine a more realistic sense of what can be accomplished in those spans.

We tend to focus on the end result of our goals rather than the process we'll need to take in order to achieve them. We know what we want, which is a good start, but the emphasis of any goal needs to be shifted towards the way in which we make it a reality. Where we're going is one thing, but we need to have a plan to get there. It's important to think about how we move towards these goals. It is equally important to gather as much information as we need in order to proceed with them. To this end, it will always be helpful to search for additional information on the subjects we'll need to familiarize ourselves with wherever we may find it.

When creating your schedule, pay careful attention to what you actually need to accomplish. Your activities should directly add to your productivity. For example, if a project you have undertaken is very likely to experience changes that will make the work you plan to do obsolete—don't include it on your schedule. Identifying and eliminating things from your daily routine that suck time away from an otherwise a productive itinerary is a good way to free up yet more time for you to do what you need to do. Also pay attention to when you are most productive.

For most of us, that will be in the morning, and much of the material in this book suggests working early and quickly, but everyone's cycle of productivity is different. While it's true that a majority of people will more greatly benefit from tackling tasks in the morning, there are plenty of people who swear by evening productivity. If that really turns out to be the case for you, then focus on major and important goals during those hours and do menial and minor tasks when you are at your least productive. To establish your times of peak productivity, it might be useful to keep up a reverse schedule, that is to say keep track of what you're doing and write it down every hour or so. You might be surprised to find after several days of this that you tend to be incredibly productive during certain periods of the day, and it's a good idea to take advantage of those times.

While most goals involve delivering a final product by a certain date, other goals require a different success metric. Say, for instance, that you're responsible for your company's blog. If you give yourself two hours a day to develop it, but only write a hundred or so words in that time-frame, you've done far less work than your 2-hour commitment implies. Give yourself a word-count or other milestone, say 1,000 words or an entire article. That way you're not just staring at the screen for most of the time, because you'll be more motivated to reach the word count or completion of the article than you would be just waiting out the clock.

In some cases, you need to forgo time-restraints in lieu of more substantial accomplishments in order to ensure that you are using our time as wisely as possible. A person who commits to write or work "for an hour" hasn't really committed to anything substantial. A person who commits to do the same, but also comes up with a word-count or more discreet measure of progress has provided a powerful internal motivational cue and will accomplish far more overall. You'll find that establishing set amounts of work you wish to complete in this fashion will keep you moving far quicker than would otherwise be feasible. If you need to keep up on a certain amount of correspondence, for example, set out specific goals for that correspondence (what e-mails need to say, where they go, and who should be included in the discussion).

A highly recommended way to go about your day is to perform your least desired task as soon as possible. Get the things you like doing the least out of your way in order to continue on with your day, and you'll experience less stress. This will take practice to start, but eventually you'll come to look forward to getting through the hard work early. The rest of your day will become easier, and you'll stop worrying about getting around to it. As you might suspect, this makes completing the remainder of your daily tasks that much easier. Without those large or otherwise imposing assignments hanging over our heads, we can proceed with far less anxiety involved.

Group similar tasks together in your schedule. Don't skip between conferencing and e-mailing and other things you need to do unless there is a very clear reason for doing so. This will allow you to build momentum as you complete each type of task individually. You can pace yourself in this fashion and save loads of time that would otherwise be spent simply switching back and forth between things you need to do. You'll find that this habit comes easily after a while. If we once attempted our work days in a somewhat less than organized fashion, we likely just tackled projects or assignments as they came to us or as we remembered they needed to be done. A schedule that has grouped similar tasks together on it will allow us to quickly move from one thing to the next, as opposed to stopping and considering what needs to get done once we've completed something else.

Just as you pay attention to when you are at your most productive, be sure to take note of when your ability to perform work wanes. For most of us, this will be some time after lunch. Believe it or not, it often has to do with what we eat for lunch. Lean meats, lots of vegetables, and legumes are a good way to stay energized. If you find yourself half-awake or nearly dozing off, that's a good sign that five or so minutes of simple stretching is in order. This will get your blood flowing again, and you'll be able to finish your day more strongly than if you'd simply tried to power through the fatigue with whatever you were presently trying to accomplish.

Enemies of Time Savings

Listed below are two activities that greatly hinder workplace productivity. Each of these activities shares a great deal in common with the next, and all of them are forms of wasting time. As you read each section, be looking for things that you do personally, and make note of how you might eliminate the unwanted habit or activity.

Procrastination: The bane of productivity. Procrastination is so commonplace that many of us are admit to regularly putting off tasks or assignments almost without noticing we do so. Any challenge or task we are loath to commit our work time to is likely to be put off for as long as possible, if not indefinitely. In the short term, procrastination is a nuisance to ourselves and those who depend on us and count on our work.

Unfortunately, procrastination has a more insidious side. If we delay what we need to do as long as possible and leave organizing until the last minute, we find ourselves in the midst of an almost insurmountable heap of disorganization. Accumulated disorder is actually quite damaging to our psyches, and those of us who tend to be on the messy personality side can easily be discouraged by how much messier things can get when we don't attend to them directly. This danger is well-understood by organized people. In fact they often remark with confusion about how their less-cleanly functioning companions or friends manage to let things get so far unraveled!

Unaddressed procrastination can have devastating consequences for the long-term.. Psychologists and other health-care professionals have known for decades that as we approach the ends of our lives, we regret the things we haven't managed. Our reflections are not filled with remorse at the things we managed to accomplish, but the things we never set out to do in the first place. The leading cause of these unachieved goals? They were put off indefinitely. For whatever reason, the motivation to do something about accomplishing them never set in.

You owe it to yourself to limit these

regrets as much as humanly possible, and it is very possible to do so. Procrastination generally sets in because we want to avoid the displeasure of completing a task (note your personality type!) and possible failure.

Sometimes, as we visualize how we would complete a task, we begin to feel a vague anxiety about engaging in that activity. Though vague, it is a powerfully motivating force — suddenly we yearn to do anything other than the task we just imagined doing. If the task has a deadline, it grows nearer and nearer until we're forced to do a frenzied and slipshod job. This often leads to failure, which in turn reinforces the idea that the task is unpleasant to begin with. The next time you are faced with such a task, you'll experience the same feelings of dread.

It's a funny quirk of human nature that we often do a poor job due to a self-imposed time-crisis. (Remember writing lengthy high school or college papers entirely the night before they were due?) Then, we blame our mad scramble on some external failure instead of our own procrastination. We may even be consciously aware that we could have done a much better job if we only hadn't avoided the task, yet *still* manage to take the failure personally and allow it to inhibit our productivity in the future. In order to overcome procrastination, we first have to separate our actions and mistakes from ourselves.

To begin with, it's a good idea to take a look at the difference between optimism and pessimism. We'll see the role this plays in procrastination almost immediately. Say, for instance, that you've reached the extent of your professional career and need to undertake new courses or perhaps earn a higher degree in order to advance. A pessimist will take one look at the course requirements and time commitments needed to accomplish this goal and bemoan fate. A commitment of two years or more under a rigorous academic routine seems impossible. A pessimist sees all of this discomfort and stress at once and backs away.

Now, to the pessimist, it might seem like the opposite person would simply charge forward and take on everything at once without hesitation. Optimists do, after all, seem to maintain an incredible can-do attitude, even in the face of incredible stress. But the reality of an optimistic point of view is really more subtle than that.

An optimist doesn't see the same challenge as a pessimist. In this case, a positive thinker doesn't immediately retreat from academic advancement because the entirety of it seems impossible. An optimist will face such an incredible task by breaking it down into steps. They recognize that just because the energy that must be spent entering and taking new courses will be massive, it won't be all at once, and it can be done in steps.

In other words, the first thing that comes into the mind of an optimist isn't necessarily (in fact, probably isn't) — *I can do this, no problem!* Instead, it is far more likely something like — *So, how do I break this down into manageable steps?* The optimist makes sure the next step is something he or she can integrate into life, while the pessimist becomes overwhelmed by all the steps at once. This simple, yet subtle, skill of breaking down colossal responsibilities into discreet and manageable steps is vital to increasing your own productivity. Every big dream you have can be accomplished by breaking that dream down into several dozen or perhaps even a hundred smaller and discreet stages. These stages form the foundation of the dream becoming your reality.

Try this simple way of managing your thoughts the next time you are faced with what appears to be a large task: ask yourself what the very first thing you need to do in order to accomplish it is, then set to doing that without paying attention to the larger goal. Nothing that requires long periods of time ever needs to be accomplished at once, so why should we allow ourselves to feel all of the accompanying stress at the outset? By making the practice of dealing with tasks in smaller chunks a habit, we can vastly increase our productivity. Maybe the optimist winds up in school for another couple of years, for example, but when time for advancement comes, the pessimist has not done the work because they have found it too daunting.

Procrastination can also come in the opposite form. Perhaps you've found the perfect way to manage those huge tasks in the office, but little ones — responding to e-mail or following up with clients — manage to slip away from you constantly. Here, the procrastinator likely doesn't feel particularly overwhelmed by the task. Rather, it may be seen as a nuisance or something unnecessary when all is said and done. A person who dislikes returning calls may not even be aware of why he or she tends not to do it.

If this is the case, another thought experiment may be called on. Here, take something small, perhaps a weekly work task that you commonly forget to accomplish on time. Now, make the commitment to do it *far more often than you need to* in the space of one week. If you dislike responding to e-mail and know it should be done on a weekly basis but manage to forget it regularly enough that you (or perhaps your employers) has a problem with it, resolve, for one week, to respond to every e-mail you receive at work, even if it is just a notice that you have received the e-mail.

Focus on a single task in one week. Remember, we may desire a wide range of changes to our productivity, but the rule of optimism implores us to break things downs, lest we become overwhelmed. Commit to tackling that task far more times than you would reasonably need to in a week. You may even feel a little silly while you're doing this — that's great. Make it a game, consider it practice, and once a successful week is finished, be sure to reflect on it with playful pride. It will be far easier to remember tasks you've tackled like this than it was before.

Remember, choose *one task only*. A week-long commitment to two or more tasks is less likely to be successful, since you will be far more likely to get bored, annoyed, or forgetful with several. Consider, for example, if you are supposed to come up with a weekly report on some project or another. Writing the entire report every day would be a clear waste of time, especially because much of the report's content probably depends on what happens throughout the week. A good way to tackle this problem, then, would be to set aside time every day to write as much as you can. This would be your focus for the week—no other changes to your work habits should occur.

Procrastination has an almost ephemeral quality to it at times. Often, we just need to *do it* instead of thinking about doing it. This previous exercise is meant to familiarize ourselves with the reality that a task we reflexively avoid because it is unpleasant or for other reasons, is actually not so bad at all. The tasks we complete regularly at work likely aren't difficult if we've been there for a while, but our perception of them can be something akin to a battle that never ends. This is often because we put off mildly unpleasant routines until they have grown daunting. A regular habit of completing simple tasks here and there is far less time-consuming. The trick is simply to stay constant in our completion of the task.

As strange as it may sound, procrastination can arise from our fear of success just as much as it can from a fear of failure. We feel that the more we accomplish, the more we will be burdened with responsibility. Here, it's up to you to make a decision. If you feel that you really do know you wouldn't desire a given outcome, ask yourself why the goal is important in the first place. If the nuisance of new responsibility really isn't worth achieving something you thought you wanted, you still won't know whether or not you can accomplish it. For many of us, it's that question that can push us forward, whatever the consequences may be.

Besides, progress towards your goals is always a learning experience. It's unlikely that you'll be unable to handle any additional responsibilities afforded to you by your accomplishment, given the amount of time and resources you spent learning it in the first place.

If you're unsure of exactly why you're procrastinating on a given project or task, and this will happen from time to time, make an effort to figure it out. Sit down and identify what it is you want out of the completion of the goal. Once you've determined what you want ultimately out of a goal, take a look at things that might stand in your way. Not all resources are tangible. You might be procrastinating on a project because you don't know how to proceed with it. If this is the case, you'll need to find someone who knows how to do it and proceed from there. Breaking tasks down in this way can draw attention to areas of personal strength that we need to develop in order to make it a reality. Often times, if we can find the reasons we're putting off a task, we can address those reasons directly and then proceed far less hindered by doubt.

Time-distortion: another rampant productivity-eater in the workplace. If we're checking e-mails at undetermined intervals throughout the day and responding to them, each time we open up our inbox, it may feel like we've only spent several minutes checking and responding to whatever comes our way. If we check our inbox and find a response to our previous e-mail, we'll respond to that—and so on and so forth. The end result is hours in a given day used up in responding to a series of similar questions or issues. It's great to remain in contact with everyone on a project, but overdoing it can lead to critical loss of time better spent on completing your objectives. Tasks like this can tear through our productive efforts if we let them, and the trick will be—and this will be very tricky at first, since things like e-mail are so popular in no small way because they are so convenient and easy to access—to establish a single time of day where you sit down and complete your correspondence. Morning will work best. It will ensure that you have time to respond to everyone and give you the rest of the day to complete everything else you need to do. It's a good idea to structure your day so that you complete these types of tasks (e-mail, phone-calls, faxes) as early as possible and then move on with your own productive efforts. Whatever projects you need to focus on can then be tackled without distraction through the rest of the day.

We can also lose time rapidly in our own minds. We might sit ourselves down with the intention of doing something, but become easily distracted (especially in front of a computer with internet access) or begin daydreaming. Perhaps we engage in something other than what we'd intended to entirely. If our goals aren't clear to us, or we haven't allotted an appropriate amount of time to sit down and direct ourselves towards their completion, we aren't using our time to its fullest. A few suggestions for combating time-distortion are listed below. Generally, they require an understanding of how we intend to use our time before we begin a given task or portion of a goal.

There are twenty-four hours in a given day. Generally, we spend eight at work, but commit a great deal more time to it than that, especially if we are serious about getting ahead in the workplace. The strategies listed below are useful for increasing the value of the time we are able to spend at work.

Motivation is Key to Productivity

Motivation and persistence are a must for any successful change in your productivity. They are as necessary here as for any other goal, and by themselves can be difficult skills to acquire, at least on the outset. Staying motivated to remain productive can represent the largest challenge to actually being productive, especially because the practice is constantly being hindered by situations and circumstances beyond our control.

Perhaps you've had this experience: having just made the singular resolution to increase your productivity in the workplace on every front, you suddenly become sick. This leads to an inability to get much of anything done and as a result, you vent your frustration on yourself. It's all too easy to take the reality of our limitations personally. Once we do this, our productivity will fall with our expectations, even though we've experienced something that genuinely limits what we can accomplish – and the effect should be only very temporary.

Another common experience is to suddenly undergo a brief but amazing burst of productivity. For some reason, we're suddenly hitting everything on our to-do list, and hitting it swiftly. This might last for a few days, but once the weekend lets up, we go back to work bereft of that determination. Again, it's easy to let ourselves become discouraged, and a discouraged mindset will hinder our abilities to progress.

For this reason, it is important for us to be forgiving of circumstances. Acknowledgement and adherence to a set of rules regarding our own personal "guilt machines" is certainly in order, because we will inevitably suffer setbacks related to ingrained laziness or unforeseen events. When this happens, we can't let that knee-jerk reaction of guilt or apathy derail us further by causing us to avoid our tasks. Instead, it will be important for us to develop skills that prevent us from succumbing to our own negativity. For anything we set out to do in the workplace, we must bear in mind that we will always have limited resources at our disposal in a given time frame, and because we're working on managing those timeframes as efficiently as possible, we're bound to run into small problems here and there. Below are several things to remember when developing habits of increased productivity regarding your general attitude towards it.

You're Trying

That's not anything to dismiss lightly. You're making an effort to become more productive. Say, for instance, you write down a schedule for yourself, but arrive at work and have either forgotten to bring it with you or cannot bring yourself to complete some of the very first tasks. (We'll get into combating morning-moods later.) Remember the difference between optimists and pessimists? Here, the pessimist comes home at the end of the day, sees the list, and grows overwhelmed with guilt at what he perceives to be failure. The optimist sees the list and thinks, "I wasn't able to do the things on my list today, but I wrote out my schedule, and that's better than nothing." The optimist will proceed to examine the list and determine what should happen next in order to make the schedule a success. The pessimist hasn't even tried, because he or she hasn't bothered to break anything down at all. The difference between positive and negative thinking really is that simple. Maybe you can't do an entire task one day at work, but there has to be something of it that can get done. Figure out something reasonable, go for it, and work your way toward its completion.

The Morning Self

As stated earlier, it's a good idea to make to the office early to avoid the rush. Many of us go to sleep with the best intentions for the next morning. We plan to wake up early and start the day off without a hitch. Upon beginning to write out schedules designed to enhance our workplace productivity, we'll resolve to get up an hour earlier and get a head-start on all of the things we need to do. In the morning, six or seven o'clock rolls around and as our alarm begins to blare, we suddenly lose interest. Perhaps you're thinking it's time to get up and start coffee, but you're imagining it and lose all interest in doing so. Like you've done with your major goals or big dreams, break the task down. What's the first thing you need to do in order to get out of bed and start your day? It will help greatly if you can remind yourself of something highly motivating, something that you enjoy doing (for many of us this will be coffee first thing in the morning) and allow that to motivate yourself. But, if that fails, then what should we do?

The short-term answer is: get moving. Sit up if you can. If you can't, move your arms or legs until you're ready to sit up. If you can't move your arms or legs, wiggle your fingers or toes —anything to try and increase circulation. Take deep breaths, get oxygen to your brain, and work towards sitting up, and eventually getting out of bed. This is no small task, especially on the mornings after nights when we've stayed awake longer than we should. Remember, you'll lose a key advantage to increased productivity in the workplace if you don't arrive early enough to get a head start on the day.

After you're out of bed, and again especially if you've had somewhat less sleep than you need, it's likely you'll be combating morning stiffness. The most effective way to fight this off is more stretching, especially your upper and lower back. This is a good time to exercise briefly. It may seem or feel like a ludicrous proposition first thing in the morning, but it is common knowledge amongst morning joggers that such physical activity in the morning can benefit one throughout the entire day in a wide range of ways. If you try it, remember to stretch and perhaps walk a little first, but your morning-sluggishness will dissolve in a matter of minutes for certain. If you're headed straight to work, you won't have time for a full jog, but five minutes or so of stretching should limber you up.

While we are on the subject of waking early and well, let's address getting to sleep early. Our mental acuity in the morning far surpasses that in the evening, after we get over the grogginess, that is. We are more likely to complete tasks we've committed to before the demands of the day set in and we find our resolve flagging. This is not true for absolutely everyone.

Some people are genuine night-owls who are most productive at night, but even if you think this might be the case with you, take a more careful look to be sure. Do you stay up later to get more done, or are you up later because you spend lots of time leisurely before going to sleep? If the latter is the case, consider sacrificing some of that time in order to get more rest.

As difficult as some early morning wake up alarms may be, it can be equally difficult for us to go to sleep at night. This is especially true if we aren't much for physical activity or something is weighing on our minds. A steady sleep schedule is vital to productivity because a person who tries to go to sleep at ten but lies awake for an hour or two has lost both that time to himself for the evening and is likely to suffer a similar loss in the morning. Many of us commit to lying down and waiting for sleep to set in. However, if sleep fails to come to you within twenty minutes of lying down, it's a good idea to get out of bed and engage in some mild activity. Don't watch TV in order to fall asleep though. Instead, listen to music, read, or clean something that can be easily cleaned. After you've done this, try to sleep again. By doing this, you are trying to get your body out of the habit of lying awake in your bed, which it may unconsciously be highly accustomed to if it takes you a while to fall asleep at night. Breaking that habit will do wonders for both your health and your productivity. By this same token, taking on what you perceive as your most unpleasant task the very first thing in the morning will make it more likely that you actually do so. If you get the hardest part of your day out of the way before anything else, then you've taken a big step towards defeating procrastination in general. Wake up, power through it, and everything else is easier than the first thing you did.

Go for It Anyway

Another strategy for ratcheting up your productivity when you feel yourself slowing or becoming tired is to simply power through it!

Often times, we misjudge because we feel that our exhaustion will make us to fail to complete tasks as well as we should. You probably won't be surprised to learn that an overwhelming amount of the energy you expend towards the completion of almost any task is required by the very last details of that task. While this might seem like a marathoner's "Heartbreak Hill," it's important to keep this phenomenon in perspective.

Our brains are much better at summing up and providing a range of estimates for simple tasks with few steps. When a task/goal contains several stages, we're far more likely to misjudge the amount of time it will take to complete the task. We might leave out a step in our planning or not realize that additional steps are necessary. Thus, as we proceed, we may find ourselves flagging as we realize how much more time it has taken than we originally thought it would.

For projects with no other value than your own sense of professional accomplishment, this can have two outcomes.

- First, because no one other than you depends upon the task's completion, you likely won't feel a sense of dread or anxiety (although frustration is common enough in these situations).

- Secondly, without some external force to drive us toward the completion of a task, we're at somewhat of a loss to find reasons to continue. In this case, we simply need to pick up our spirits and power through the task at hand. That is, if we determine that our sense of self-worth is valuable enough, and it is always valuable enough! We may take pains to establish deadlines for projects we've undertaken in the workplace, but they hold little value if no one else is holding us to those deadlines especially if your professional life is already hectic.

For projects that *are* critical to your professional success, flagging may involve only one detail:

- Anxieties brought about by deadlines are highly motivating. We may be able to shake a goal off by telling ourselves that we don't feel like doing it, but try having a similar conversation with your boss at work and you'll see the difference.

"Go For it Anyway" may be easier said than done, or you wouldn't be reading this book in the first place. It's easy enough to say it, but *how*? Perhaps you've read books on the subject of motivation, and they gave you helpful pointers that helped you every now and then. Unfortunately, more often than not, much of the literature on the subject can miss a very simple and very significant fact about motivation; all the explanations and rationalization on the subject amount to almost nothing, because it isn't the rational thinking centers in our brain that have a major impact on our motivation. We aren't driven to do things that we think about regularly, we are driven to do things we *feel* strongly about.

Motivation is not a logical process — it is an emotional one. It is the development of new emotional outlooks, not rational understanding, that will push us forward. We're not teaching ourselves new ways of thinking — at least, the work doesn't stop there — what we need to do in order to become more productive, is to change the ways in which we *feel*. Strange that in so many works in self-development the emphasis rests on the cognitive thinking processes rather than the emotive or motivational affectations they are designed to. Changing the way you think isn't a bad idea by any means if the outcome is to increase motivation, but if a thought-process you've adopted or are trying to incorporate isn't working, it's time to move on to something else and see if that works.

Be Ready for "Failure"

Setbacks, complications, and time-constraints happen. While we can adopt strategies to minimize them, they will not disappear, and it will seem initially that your efforts toward increased productivity will become mired in them. If and when you begin to feel hopeless, be advised: everyone who has ever or will go down this path will feel this way. You will feel frustrated sometimes, hopeless now and then, and even defeated on occasion.

It's hard for nearly all of us to adjust our expectations to appropriate levels in this manner. We might feel that we should be in control of absolutely everything, but that will simply never be the case. Expect to increase your productivity through a constant series of trials-and-errors, with the emphasis on errors. The errors represent lessons, and the first and longest lesson we'll have to learn is what we can actually accomplish in a single day. It may seem like very little at first, and it will be difficult to gauge what you've managed to learn with each challenge you face, but even if you don't notice it, your productivity will increase by simply reframing hang-ups or setbacks in terms of learning experiences. If a situation was in your control, what could you have done to prevent a setback? If it wasn't in your control, dismiss it as such and move on to something that is.

Thought Exercises

Below are some common tips and thought exercises designed to tap into your emotional power. If you find yourself writing up a schedule every night but simply tossing it aside every morning, practice any of these techniques until you've found something that works for you. The reaction you'll be looking for will be one of sudden clarity and direction. If, for example, you decide to imagine yourself after the task is completed, that much more successful and fulfilled, your visualization of the tasks completion will take on a vivid texture and you'll notice your heart-rate rise suddenly with enthusiasm. It's not enough to know what you should do and understand why you should do it — you have to feel it.

Make Sure It's Doable

This sounds obvious, but when faced with a task, and a sudden motivational impetus, we tend to set our sights far too high above what we can actually accomplish in the time we've allotted ourselves. Goals should always be broken down into discrete pieces that can be accomplished simply and within an hour or two. Deciding to work on a massive project for six hours at a time may seem like the best way to tackle it at first, but after the first several hundred minutes, we may find ourselves exhausted. In this case, it's a much better idea to take a break and resolve to come back to the task at a later time, when we are restored and possess a fresher perspective. Two hours of solid work on a project is better than six hours where more and more of your time is simply spent trying to push forward. If you're constantly setting up huge amounts of time for yourself and finding that you run out of time or energy quickly, you can become easily discouraged. Set up tasks for yourself where you are bound to succeed at first.

Completion-Imaging

This can be a good exercise to reinvigorate yourself midway through a task, or to bring yourself to begin something you've been putting off for a while. Close your eyes and use your imagination to visualize the task being absolutely finished. Try to give the mental image as much vivid detail as you possibly can, paying attention to the way you feel. Let yourself feel as excited as you can. Don't focus on the fact that it's just in your imagination. Instead, use that energy—the imagined enthusiasm at having finished something difficult—and imagine yourself starting that task with the very same enthusiasm.

There's a minor distinction here that becomes important in the application of this procedure. If you simply picture yourself as being enthusiastic, but don't feel any of that enthusiasm directly, you might not be able to access that emotion as well as you'll need to. If this is the case, instead of viewing the scenario in the first person at first, imagine yourself somewhat distanced from it, perhaps ten feet away. While you remain emotionally detached, watch yourself becoming more and more enthusiastic about the task as though you were watching a movie. Take as long as you feel appropriate, and then simply move your awareness into the mental image you've created of yourself. Feel your thoughts merging with the visualization, and feel the visualization's emotional processes take over your own — leaving you driven and directed toward the task at hand. You'll find quickly this is a better jump-start to your motivation for bigger tasks. Menial tasks such as chores or errands may benefit more from later exercises. This represents a basic attempt at trying to access emotions which would drive you towards a larger goal by focusing on positive end results and utilizing the potential benefits of increased productivity to your advantage.

Identify Your Strengths and Weaknesses

Come up with a list of things you consider yourself to be good at and things that you feel you still need to work on. You might be a good organizer, or great at remaining clutter-free. Perhaps you're a skilled persuader or able to understand others' points of view more readily than those around you. Do you have a knack for attention to detail? Perhaps you're better at big-picture situations, or good at being able to identify potential pitfalls and avoid them.

It's good to know your strengths, but even better to know what sorts of things you'd like to work on. If, for example, you feel you are a poor communicator, being a better one can easily become a goal for you. If you tend to collect disorganization, take several hours a week to practice cutting down on the amount of clutter or mess you generate. There's no rule anywhere that says you have to adhere to a bad habit just because you've done so in the past. That is to say, just because you do something you don't like, that doesn't mean it's a part of your personality. We're all capable of learning new skills and incorporating them into our daily lives, with sufficient motivation.

Remind Yourself of Your Successes

If you find your energy dropping due to lack of confidence or fear of failure, take a minute or two to recall something that you succeeded at. This will be most helpful to you if you can recall something similar to what you are currently attempting to accomplish. Mull it over and try to remember your thoughts and mindset before you were successful. Often-times, you'll discover that your way of thinking was similar then to what it is now. In this way, we can steady ourselves and move forward with whatever we need to get done.

Likewise, any time you are successful with a task, make note of it and take pride. You've just acquired another model of behavior that will help you in the future with similar tasks. You've made it that much easier for yourself when the next time comes around to accomplish a related objective. Be sure to ask yourself what made you accomplish the goal. If the answer is something like "I knew I had to do it, so I just went ahead and did it," you're on to something!

Remind yourself constantly of the things that you are good at. Draw whatever you can from your strengths—if, for example, you consider yourself a poor speaker, but have often earned praise for your ability to write clearly and concisely, consider writing out things you might need to say for tasks that require phone conversations or meetings in person. You may not actually need to read directly from your list, but the notes will help spur you along in the direction you wish to go.

Records and Rewards

Graph Your Progress

For those of you with a penchant for analyzing your progress, charting and graphing programs like Microsoft Excel can have incredible motivational power. You'll need a basic understanding of how to convert the table information into a graph, and you might want to check your progress on a daily or weekly basis. You can set an "average" amount of goals you want to complete every day, perhaps dividing them up into minor, moderate, and major ones. Be sure to try to give yourself room for improvement. You can even transfer your written schedule into an Excel chart. This has the added advantage of keeping both your progress logs in one place, because you can annotate the cells to your heart's content.

Keeping a careful record of your progress really is an excellent way to stay motivated. One of the reasons that graphs and charts are a must for business presentations and the like is that they put whatever goals your company is discussing into concrete visual layouts. You have every reason to expect that the more detailed and visually aided your own attempts at progress are, the farther you will get.

The nature of the graph itself is really up to you. As stated above, consider dividing your tasks into minor, moderate, and major goals. At the end of every day, take stock of what you've completed against what you didn't. Keep a tally of these points across time if it helps. You can check yourself against your average in this fashion. In this way, you'll also be able to establish a somewhat more objective baseline for your productivity. You'll know when you're really moving, so to speak, and when you're going slowly. Also be sure to mark times on your chart when you were disrupted, because it will help you identify times when interruptions are common. Then, you can strategize how to avoid those interruptions in the future. Mark when you are sick, when a task unexpectedly comes up, and so on. This way, you'll know when you have reasons for why you were unable to complete the tasks you'd set out for yourself, versus when you were not sufficiently motivated toward them.

Be prepared to hold onto these charts and graphs. It may sound silly, but think of it as a record of your own progress. Months and years from now, you can look back at your earlier attempts at productivity and physically see what you've accomplished since then. This is especially useful if we feel we've fallen into some kind of rut. Nothing will motivate you more in the present than suddenly remembering you've done similar or even more difficult tasks a month or two ago. You might even rediscover a way of partitioning up a task you're on the road to completing by taking a look at sufficient data from past experiences.

Keeping track of productivity in this fashion also serves as a testament to your commitment to stay on whatever path you've chosen. Think of it like an ever-growing trophy that reflects your accomplishments in time and energy well-spent. You'll be far more motivated to forgo your daily television or internet regiment if you do so.

Reward Yourself

This is an especially good motivator if you're determined to increase your earnings. Set a monetary goal for yourself — something you want to work towards making in a month or year, and agree to reward yourself with something you will *really* enjoy once you've obtained that goal. Whatever you decided to reward yourself with, make sure it doesn't exceed the money you've taken in by completing your goals, but other than that, anything is fair game. Be creative here — perhaps there's a particular vacation you've wanted to take, for example. Simply buying something as a result of your success is fine, but try to look deeper for things that will motivate you further.

BF Skinner, the founder of what is currently known as Behavioral Science, identified motivators that encouraged all kinds of behaviors. While he identified them in animals such as mice and pigeons, much of what he discovered can be applied in simple and elegant ways in order to modify human behavior. If you complete a task, and are immediately rewarded for the completion of that task, you will be more motivated toward that behavior in the future. Skinner generally used food, but here's where the advantage of being human comes in: we have a wide range of objects and activities that can reinforce our behavior. To some extent, this is why television and movies are so popular. All you need to do is turn the box on, and it provides you with as much entertainment as you want. Unfortunately, as we've already discussed, this activity drastically reduces our productivity and leads to long-term complications over time. The trick here is to establish a scheduled of set reinforcement and stick with it. Be careful not to reward yourself for something as simple as logging on to your computer or checking your correspondence with hours of wasted time. Alternatives are abundant, so think of things that you enjoy doing outside the realm of passive media and stick with those.

There are certainly worse ways to spend extra income than rewarding your dedicated effort, and it's always a good idea to foster a skill in some way that will grant monetary benefits. The money itself will prove to be a powerful reinforcer for your continued perseverance. Another important aspect of behaviorism, especially in humans, is that after a while the task itself becomes reinforcing, since it has been paired with such desirable outcomes.

Schedule Relaxation

You won't be able to work every day nonstop. Indeed, why should you? It's important to find the right balance between productivity and time that you spend unwinding and reflecting on what you've managed to accomplish. In this vein, when you're off work, make sure to stay away from work. Try to schedule an hour or two when you can switch gears and take it easy. If you have family, engage with them in some meaningful way. Walk your dog. Read from a book. Phone a friend or family member you haven't spoken to in a while.

Do take time to consider what activities (aside from television) genuinely relax you. It's also a good idea to use some of this time for power-naps. Fifteen minutes or so spent generally relaxing and thinking things over can get things moving for you again at the end of a long day. You can choose from a wide range of relaxation techniques that are proven to help people distance themselves from their workplace. This will more likely ensure that you come in the next day better prepared for whatever you've got to do. After all, if we stay stressed out and wound up from whatever we've got going on at work, we're not going to be rested up enough for it the next day. A day's work is well worth an evening of relaxation, so be sure to take advantage of the time you're not at work in order to do so in a healthy fashion.

Productivity Tips and Tricks

Decide Quickly

Have you ever reached a point in a task where you come to an unexpected decision? It's common, when presented with an unexpected problem or choice, to stop work and mull it over, but such mulling can lead to long-term delays in the completion of a task. When you come to such places, give yourself a discreet amount of time to make a decision, say twenty seconds to a full minute. Once you've made that decision, act on it and proceed with whatever you were doing. This helps avoid tying unnecessary time up in coming to a decision that you're actually just as capable of making in the moment. Feeling this need to stop is akin to procrastination. Suddenly we're not as certain how to proceed, so we feel the need to stop until something external clicks into place and we can continue. However, the decision is always ours to make, and we are best benefited by deciding quickly and moving on. You'll often find that you can begin to make these types of decisions almost immediately. You already know what you're trying to accomplish, and whatever decision you make in the instant will reflect that knowledge. If you go with your intuition, you'll generally be right.

Do a Horrible Job

Some people swear by this method. When faced with a task that provokes extreme anxiety in you, don't set out to do your best at first. Instead, do it as poorly as you can. Make fun of the task and how nervous you are at completing it. Go for it: just know that no one will ever see what you're doing, so it won't matter. Once you've finished, you can set out to complete the task in a more serious manner. You'll be surprised at how much of what you thought was terrible actually becomes the foundation for what you actually accomplish— after all, if you've done an intentionally bad job, you can only improve on it from there. Review any task you've completed and see if it's really as bad as you thought. You'll often find that you've given yourself an important foundation for whatever goal you've made for yourself. Give yourself license to make light of the task, and the completion of it may suddenly become tangible and achievable.

This is a great way to defeat the more threatening aspects of major goals and is really akin to a form of gameplay. In a sense, you're actually accomplishing the task you set out to achieve. Because it is for yourself, you don't need to worry about being afraid of failure, especially because you set out with failure in mind. Intentionally making a mess of something you want to accomplish can rearrange it for you in a way that takes the stress out of a situation.

Educate Yourself

There are books and courses and materials available for everything you could possibly want to achieve. Sites such as Amazon.com and Half.com are incredibly useful. Log on, type in the skill or hobby you're trying to cultivate, and search the results. Very likely, you won't need to go past the first page to come up with something that can help with your specific goal. There may even be classes or groups in your area dedicated to the same idea, and joining them will greatly increase your productivity and provide a very useful burst of motivation. You'll find answers to questions, simple directions to seemingly complicated problems, emotional support and further suggestions for reading or developing your goals in any one of these resources.

This is where devices such as e-readers and tablets can again come in extremely handy. Why order a book for delivery (and have it take up just that much more space when it arrives) if you can pay less for the book, nothing at all for shipping, and receive it immediately? The electronic reading revolution is still under development, but nearly any book you can buy will be cheaper in that format, and oftentimes the difference can result in long-term savings of hundreds of dollars.

You can also find an endless supply of podcasts and other electronic materials on sites like YouTube.com, and these are just clicks away from being a part of your knowledge. Many such books come out with regular updates or have associated websites and blogs attached to them. These sites can contain additional tips and pointers for anything you may wish to accomplish, and while the purchase of the book it supplements may be optimal for your productivity, it is by no means necessary if the price of the materials is higher than you'd prefer.

This is also a good way to make use of your commute, if you spend a considerable amount of time going to and from work every day. Instead of talk radio, find these materials in audio format and listen to them that way. The more you immerse yourself in the goals you've set out to accomplish, the more likely you'll be to follow through with them. This is especially useful for major goals, and people in search of success stories. You'll be surprised at how similar they are to yours at the outset. If that's true, why can't their story ultimately be yours in the end?

However you decide to build up your academic materials for the pursuits of your choice, pursue the materials one at a time. Books often make references to other books, and it's a good idea to keep yet another list of materials you may need in the future. Do be sure to finish reading (and taking notes) from one book at a time. It's always important to keep your attention directed to one aspect of a goal at a time. Once you've finished it, go back and look at your notes. Use your intuition to tell you what you need more information on next, and look for something on that subject.

Multitasking

This form of task management involves the completion of two (or perhaps three, but that's unlikely) objectives that can be completed simultaneously. While this will almost guarantee that either task is completed more slowly than it would be if you'd completed it on its own, for menial tasks that do not require dedicated effort to accomplish, multitasking can allow you to complete two tasks in less time than if you'd done them one after the other.

The idea of multitasking on significant goals may seem appealing, but it's important to know that research throughout the 1990s on the concept revealed that it is not a good method to adopt when tackling larger projects. Anything that requires a modicum of planning or preparation is not a good candidate for simultaneous completion with something else. For example, if you try to maintain a phone conversation while designing a new piece of furniture, you'll be distracted and unable to focus on either task. It's important to understand our psychological limitations regarding multi-tasking, so that we don't try to double up on things that will require our full attention. Doing so will waste time and resources that would be better directed at one project at a time. Multitasking is a good skill to develop for management positions where your attention may be required to go in many directions at once, but if you're entering data or trying to accomplish something with even a modicum of finesse required, stay focused on one thing at a time.

Don't Let it Get to You

Don't let failures, delays, or just plain misfortune get to you. Admittedly, the practice of shaking off bad luck or speed-bumps along that way is difficult. Each of us inherently knows that we're capable of more than we are presently accomplishing. When we encounter things that are simply beyond our control we can quickly leap to an emotional conclusion that it was somehow our fault the task was not completed correctly or on time. If something goes wrong, look at why it may have gone wrong and try to distance it from your sense of self-worth. Look at the situation as objectively as possible and run it by someone you trust if necessary.

We believe we're capable of more than we presently accomplish because we are. When things get in the way, allow yourself to accept a temporary setback without succumbing to feelings of total failure. Things do happen on a regular basis that will necessarily distract us from our goals. It's important to stay committed to these goals and ensure that they are only frustrated in the moment.

It's a good practice to keep trying and working through problems precisely when these feelings seem like they are about to overwhelm you. We have a tendency to anchor ourselves in previous expectations. For an easy example, try walking across a surface six inches wide, raised just a few feet off the ground. If this sounds doable, that's because it would be an easy accomplishment for almost anyone. Take that same plank, however, and set it between two rooftops several hundred feet in the air, and suddenly the possibility of failure seems much greater, even if we haven't changed the actual task.

So much of our behavior is the result of acting on previous beliefs and assumptions that a simple change in those assumptions can lead to progress. It was long thought that no airplane could ever surpass the speed of sound: researchers insisted that the resonating stress involved in such great velocities would tear any plane apart. In fact, the first plane to break the sound barrier suddenly stopped shuddering and travelled far smoother than it had under the barrier. Likewise, experts thought that a human being could never run anything fast than a four minute mile. Several decades ago, when this barrier was broken, the feat was suddenly repeated hundreds of times over in a short period of time. In the 60s and 70s, leading computer industry experts found the idea of people having the machines in their homes downright laughable.

Negative and positive emotions are both affected by this type of anchoring. This is great for positive emotions, because they naturally direct us toward what we want in life. For negative emotions, however, they can only hold us back, and that means these beliefs are harmful to our productivity. No change will be immediate. You'll likely feel frustrated in many of your goals for time to come, but gradual change is inevitable in the face of constant attempts made to do so. Whatever your personal setbacks may be, recognize that you are trying to move forward, and in trying, you are slowly succeeding, even if that feeling of success isn't always accessible.

The ancient Greeks told the story of Orpheus, who descends into the underworld to retrieve his beloved Eurydice. Hades agrees to release her, on the grounds that Orpheus does not turn around to see if her spirit is actually following him on his way out. He travels the entire distance back to the above world without glancing behind himself, until he reaches the cavern exit and is plagued by a terrible doubt. He hasn't seen or heard Eurydice since he began his journey. He believes he has been duped by Hades, and as he turns around, he sees the shade of his life's love fade back into the darkness, never to be seen again. Two more steps, perhaps one, and he would have achieved his goal.

Lucky for us, the Greeks were pessimistic in their appraisal of the human spirit. Whatever goals you have will not suddenly vanish into the darkness the moment you begin to doubt. They can, however, become unduly suspended by our disbelief. If we let these doubts prey on our motivations sufficiently, they can delay our accomplishments indefinitely, and that is a situation we should all strive to avoid. We do, after all, owe ourselves the full effort and attention required of our best and biggest dreams.

Move Through It

As much as you should limit the ability negative emotions have on you from completing a task, you should be just as willing to continue with your goals in the face of whatever stress or anxieties you are experiencing. Recognize your fear of failure or success as such, and make an effort (and it can be quite an effort at times) to finish your goal anyway. If you're anxious, uncertain, whatever the case may be, if you can find a way to get started, you're likely to experience a big reduction in whatever emotions you may be experiencing that block you from moving forward. If you feel those emotions on the rise again suddenly, it might be a good idea to make an effort to control your breathing as much as possible. This in itself can often help reduce anxiety and focus the mind on whatever you need it to.

The best way to begin this practice is by choosing small tasks that hold little value for you, but may nonetheless be completed. Tackle these little ones first, and move on to big ones once you know you can do it. Major tasks in life will always require greater effort and focus of us, and we're more likely to follow through with something we want to accomplish if we ultimately feel confident that we can do it. Remember, when something appears to be overwhelming, the trick is to find a way to break it down. Don't attempt something you can't possibly manage, instead find a small piece or aspect of the task that is manageable and run with it. Don't allow yourself to become overwhelmed by what you think you can't do, because the odds are that you can do it, but you just need to design a roadmap of some sort that will get you there.

De-clutter

The ability to stay organized and mess-free is a goal for many of us in and of itself. When paper tends to pile up around us, we're less likely to feel motivated around it. A clean workspace, on the other hand, can give us the impetus and mental focus we need in order to direct ourselves through almost anything. The more organized the tools of your trade, the faster you will be able to find anything you might need.

To this end, if you find clutter piling up about you, set to work on your belongings with large plastic bags. Find your nearest goodwill and start making trips. If something can't be used, throw it away or recycle it. Think about getting rid of objects you haven't used in a year or so: consider whether or not they really have enough sentimental value to hold on to. Chances are, you won't even notice that they're gone.

De-cluttering can become one of the minor goals you incorporate into your schedule. In fact, if you devote as little as ten minutes a day to this type of organizational activity, results will accumulate quickly. Choose a room, and get to work on it. There will be no need to set specific objectives here. All you need to do is start getting rid of clutter in that particular area until it's gone. Simply set out to remove anything you don't need from the space. Be prepared to give it away if you can, or throw it away if the object is no longer usable. Attack closet spaces, cupboards and the like to free up the most space —that's where most of the things we never get around to using wind up.

To prevent further clutter from invading your space while you're trying to take care of the problem, try to remove one or two pieces of clutter from your home for every new object that comes in. Take a look at your wardrobe—are there things in there you haven't worn in eight months, or perhaps a year? Take a look at your dishes, and see if there are any chipped or cracked that can reasonably be thrown out. How many bottles of Windex or other cleaning supplies do you have in your house? Look at your bookshelf and determine if you'll ever read certain books again. The answer is almost certainly no, and they'll do more good donated to a public library than they will taking up space in your home. Productivity and organization go hand in hand, just as much as disorder and apathy. By getting rid of anything that's unnecessary, you're helping yourself maintain a positive attitude.

A Final Note

Motivation and productivity go hand in hand, as do dedication and organization. There's no way around the obstacles presently keeping you from your goals but through them. Your efforts to increase professional productivity will consist of an ongoing process that causes you to evaluate and eliminate old and inefficient habits in order to replace them with new ones. Changing a habit is a major accomplishment, and should be rewarded as such. Succumbing to the old habits, however, must be expected. We won't be able to transform ourselves overnight into productivity-driven machines. Take great care not to beat yourself up mentally for minor slip-ups now and then. In fact, don't even take major slip-ups or perceived failures to heart. Doing so won't help you get where you're going. The only thing that can help you accomplish that is your own persistence and active attempts at striving forwards.

When you set out towards a goal, don't expect the goal to get easier. Instead, expect your ability to achieve that goal to become stronger. Increasingly, your professional productivity will become a testament to your character and ability to achieve. Taking interest in the information and resources above proves that you are at the very least interested in doing so. Now it's time to figure out how interested in it you really are.

Develop your own personal style. For goal-setting and scheduling, are you a spiral-bound notebook sort of personality? Maybe you prefer word-processing programs on a computer, or binders that will easily allow you to rearrange information and notes on your progress. For your workspace — and a good goal if you don't have a workspace is to get one — choose the style that fits you best. If you're motivated by visual images, do you prefer Escher or Rembrandt? If you find yourself collecting quotes on your subject matter, try to determine if you prefer humorous quips as opposed to spiritual musings or vice versa, as another example. This book can give you an outline of the procedures and techniques you can use to adjust your time-usage and hopefully provide tips at fostering emotional well-being in the process, but it will be up to you to determine your own style.

Don't be afraid to get quirky. Successful and productive types often are. This is because they are more comfortable with asserting themselves in the presence of adversity, and have grown far more accustomed to dealing with failures and setbacks than we presently know to be possible. But, it is possible, given time and patience.

Einstein once remarked to a student who was experiencing difficulty in the subject of mathematics that he shouldn't worry, because Einstein's own difficulties in the subject were infinitely greater. Perhaps he was making a playful remark meant to play on the difficulties of the work he was presently engaged in, but there's a far more likely meaning behind what he said. The theory of general relativity changed the way people viewed the world almost the moment it was released. Einstein himself had, prior to his sudden worldwide renown as the greatest scientist who had ever lived, suffered from extraordinary feelings of self-doubt and hopelessness. His entire life, his teachers, peers, and nearly everyone around him, had perceived him as unremarkable, uninteresting, and below average.

Most of us would be happy to change the world to a mere fraction of the degree accomplished by Einstein. We can take his statement about his difficulty in mathematics and apply it to anything we wish to achieve in life. Whatever we set out to do, there is likely already someone who has faced our very same challenge with even more doubt and uncertainty, and accomplished it nonetheless.

Visit

EmpowermentNation.com

to view other fantastic books,

sign up for book alerts, giveaways, and updates!

CPSIA information can be obtained
at www.ICGtesting.com
Printed in the USA
FSOW03n0934050217
30423FS

9 781495 915635